The Eight Nights of
Hanukkah

BY JUDY NAYER • ILLUSTRATED BY YURI SALZMAN

Consultant: Rabbi Rachel Rembrandt
Temple Beth Haverim, Mahwah, New Jersey

Troll

This edition published in 2001.

A CREATIVE MEDIA APPLICATIONS PRODUCTION

Art Direction by Fabia Wargin Design

Copyright © 1998 by Creative Media Applications.

Published by WhistleStop, an imprint and registered trademark of Troll Communications L.L.C.

Printed in the United States of America.

ISBN 0-8167-4550-1

10   9   8   7   6   5   4   3

The First Night

At last, Hanukkah is here! Tonight is the first night. I'm Rebecca, and my family and I are getting ready to celebrate. Dad gets the menorah. Mom and I clean and polish it until it shines. My little brother, Josh, finds the candles. Then we wait for sundown.

The sun has set. It is finally time to light the menorah.

Dad is going to let me light the first candle, all by myself! First, he lights the shammas. That's the helper candle that lights all the others.

Dad hands the shammas to me. Very carefully, I use it to light the first Hanukkah candle. Mom and Dad recite the blessings in English and Hebrew. We put the menorah in front of the window so everyone will see our Hanukkah lights.

After dinner, Josh and I open the first of our Hanukkah presents. We both get new backpacks! We'll get another present from our parents each night, although not every family celebrates this way.

Lighting the Candles

On each of the eight nights of Hanukkah, candles are lit at sundown. On the first night, the shammas is used to light one candle. Each night the shammas lights another candle, until all eight candles and the shammas are lit together. These blessings are said each night when the candles are lit.

Praised be Thou, O Lord our God,
King of the Universe,
Who has sanctified us with His commandments
And commanded us to kindle the Hanukkah lights.

Ba-ruch a-ta A-do-nai,
El-o-hey-nu me-lech ha-o-lam,
a-sher kid'sha-nu b'mitz-vo-tav,
v'tzee-va-nu l'had-lik ner shel Ha-nuk-kah.

Praised be Thou, O Lord our God,
King of the Universe,
Who performed miracles for our ancestors
In days of old at this season.

Ba-ruch a-ta A-do-nai,
El-o-hey-nu me-lech ha-o-lam,
she-asa nee-seem la-a-vo-tey-nu
ba-ya-mim ha-hem ba-z'man haz-zeh.

MAKING A MENORAH

The menorah is the special candleholder used during Hanukkah. There are many different kinds of menorahs, but each has a place for eight candles—one for each night of Hanukkah—and the shammas candle. Here is a menorah you can make yourself.

MATERIALS: a piece of wood (about 3" x 12"), glue, blue paint, paintbrush, silver glitter, 11 large metal nuts. Be sure the nuts are the right size to hold the Hanukkah candles snugly.

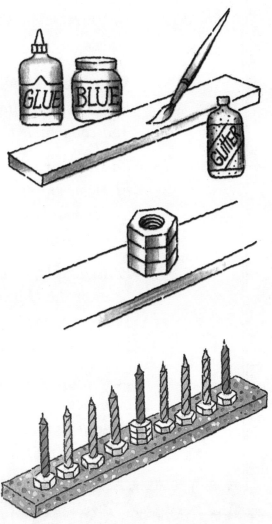

1. Mix a little glue into the paint and paint the wood blue. Before the paint dries, sprinkle the wood with glitter.

2. To make the shammas holder, stack and glue three nuts together. Glue them to the center of the piece of wood.

3. For the other candles, glue four nuts on each side of the shammas holder. Be sure to space out the nuts evenly.

The Second Night

Tonight is the second night of Hanukkah. Josh uses the shammas to light two candles. Then Dad tells us the story of Hanukkah.

"A long, long time ago, in the land of Judea, the Jewish people lived peacefully. They believed in only one God and prayed in a beautiful Temple in Jerusalem. But when a Syrian king named Antiochus became ruler, everything changed. He said the Jewish people should pray to many gods, as he did. He said the Jewish religion was not allowed.

"One day, the king's soldiers traveled to the Jewish town of Modin. They asked a wise old man named Mattathias to bow down to a statue of one of their gods. Mattathias refused. This made King Antiochus furious. He sent his men to destroy the Temple of Jerusalem and to punish any Jews who would not obey him.

7

"All might have been lost if it had not been for Mattathias and his five sons. They gathered a small band of Jews to fight back. The oldest son, Judah, became their leader. He trained the men to be soldiers, and soon they had a small army.

"And do you know what they were called?" asks Dad.

"The Maccabees!" I shout.

"That's right," says Dad. "They were so strong they were called the Maccabees, the Hebrew word for 'hammers.'

"The king's army was huge. It had thousands of soldiers. But the Maccabees were clever. They hid in caves and made surprise attacks. Little by little, they began to defeat the king's army. Finally, after three long years, Antiochus's soldiers gave up.

"Judah and the Maccabees marched into Jerusalem. The people took back their Temple and began working to make it beautiful again. They cleaned and polished the wood and stone, repaired the walls, took out Antiochus's statues, and built a new altar.

"At last, the Temple was ready to be dedicated to God again. It was time to light the traditional seven-candle menorah, the symbol of the Jews' love for God. The menorah was supposed to remain lit all the time. But the people could find only a small jar of oil, enough to last for just one day. It would take eight days to make more oil. The Jews were too excited about opening their Temple again to wait. They decided to pour the oil into the lamp anyway.

"And do you know what happened?" asks Dad.

"The menorah burned for eight whole days!" I answer.

"It was a miracle!" adds Josh.

"That's right," says Dad. "It was a miracle that the oil lasted for eight days, just enough time to make more oil. And it was a miracle that a small group of soldiers could defeat a huge army."

"And that's why we celebrate eight days of Hanukkah, right?" I ask. "And that's also why we have a different Hanukkah menorah, with room for eight candles?"

"Right!" says Dad.

CELEBRATING HANUKKAH

More than 2,000 years ago, in the land that is now called Israel, Judah and the Maccabees won the fight for the Jewish people to be able to practice their religion. On the twenty-fifth day of the Hebrew month of Kislev, the Temple in Jerusalem was made holy again and dedicated to God. The Jews celebrated, and Judah declared that every year, beginning on that day, there would be an eight-day holiday. He called the holiday Hanukkah, which means "dedication."

The Hebrew calendar is different from the calendar we use. Our calendar is a solar calendar. It is based on the earth's 365-day journey around the sun. The Hebrew calendar is a lunar calendar and has been used for more than 5,000 years. It follows the moon's 29 1/2-day trip around the earth. Since twelve lunar cycles equals only 354 days, every few years an extra month is added to the Hebrew calendar so that the lunar year keeps up with the solar year. Otherwise, we might be celebrating Hanukkah in July! Since the Jewish holidays follow the Hebrew calendar, each year Hanukkah falls on different days on our calendar.

September	
October	Tishri
November	Heshvan
December	Kislev HANUKKAH
January	Tevet
February	Shevat
March	Adar
April	Nisan
May	Iyar
June	Sivan
July	Tammuz
August	Av
	Elul

Oh, Hanukkah

There are many Hanukkah songs we sing to help celebrate the holiday. "Oh, Hanukkah" is usually sung after lighting the candles.

Oh, Ha-nuk-kah, Oh, Ha-nuk-kah, come light the me-no-rah!

Let's have a par-ty, we'll all dance the ho-rah.

Gath-er 'round the ta-ble, we'll give you a treat, Shin-

ing tops to play with, and lat-kes to eat. And

while we are play-ing, the can-dles are burn-ing low.

One for each night, they shed a sweet light, To re-

mind us of days long a-go. One for each night, they

shed a sweet light, To re-mind us of days long a-go.

The Third Night

Tonight is the third night of Hanukkah. Mom and I light three candles. Then Grandma Esther comes! Every year Grandma brings her special, homemade potato pancakes. She makes the best potato pancakes in the world!

"Did you bring potato pancakes, Grandma?" I ask.

"No," Grandma answers. "This time I'm going to make my latkes right here. And you're going to help!"

Grandma takes out all the ingredients. Then we get to work. I help Grandma grate the potatoes and the onions. Then I mix in the eggs, flour, and salt.

Grandma pours some oil into a big frying pan. When the oil is hot, she spoons small amounts of the batter into the pan. I want to help with this part, but the oil is too hot.

Soon the potato pancakes are crispy and brown on both sides. Grandma lifts them out of the pan with a spatula and puts them on paper towels to drain.

The latkes smell yummy. I can't wait to eat them! Grandma doesn't make me wait. She gives me a bowl of applesauce to dip them in, and I take a taste. Mmmmm!

MAKING LATKES

Potato pancakes (*latkes* in Yiddish) are a favorite Hanukkah treat. During Hanukkah, we fry latkes in oil to remind us of the miracle of the oil that burned for eight days. Ask a grownup to help you make these latkes.

INGREDIENTS: 6 large potatoes, 2 small onions, 2 eggs, 4 tablespoons flour, 1 teaspoon salt, vegetable oil

1. Soak the potatoes in a bowl of water for about half an hour. Then drain and peel them.

2. Grate the potatoes and onions using a metal grater or food processor. Put them into a large bowl, pouring off any extra liquid.

3. Add the eggs, flour, and salt. Let the mixture sit for a few minutes to thicken.

4. Heat several tablespoons of oil in a large frying pan. Drop in the mixture by the tablespoon, and flatten with a spatula.

5. When the latkes are brown on the bottom, turn them over. When the other side is brown, remove them and drain them on paper towels. Serve with applesauce.

Makes about 18 medium-sized pancakes.

The Fourth Night

Tonight is the fourth night of Hanukkah. After we light the candles, Dad sends us on a treasure hunt! Josh and I search the whole house for Hanukkah gelt. *Gelt* means "money" in Yiddish. I think Dad hides the best kind of money—chocolate money! I find ten chocolate coins, all wrapped in gold foil. Josh finds seven, but Dad gives him three more so it's even.

17

Mom makes us wait until after dinner to eat our chocolate money. Then Dad says, "Now let's see if you can find some real money!" He hands me a folded piece of paper. "Here's your clue," he says. I open it up and read:

What shines and flickers in the night,
to fill the room with glowing light?

"That's easy!" I shout. "It's the menorah!" Josh and I run to the menorah on the windowsill. There is a small envelope right next to it. Inside is a five-dollar bill for each of us!

MAKING A GELT HOLDER

When the Maccabees defeated Antiochus, they threw away the coins with his picture on them. They made new coins with Judah Maccabee's picture. The tradition of giving Hanukkah gelt became part of the holiday. At first, money was given as a gift only to teachers. Later, children received gelt for Hanukkah. You can keep your gelt in this beautiful box.

MATERIALS: empty cereal box, scissors, blue construction paper, glue, stapler, gold wrappers from chocolate coins, glitter, other decorative materials

1. Cut off the top of an empty cereal box.

2. Cut blue construction paper to fit the four sides of the box. Attach with glue.

3. Cut a handle about three inches wide from construction paper. Fold the paper twice, until it is one inch wide, to make the handle stronger. Staple the handle to the box.

4. Decorate the outside of the box by gluing on gold wrappers from chocolate coins, glitter, and other materials.

5. Fill the box with chocolate coins to have as a treat for guests. Or use the box to collect money for charity.

The Fifth Night

Tonight is the fifth night of Hanukkah. After we light the candles, Mom, Dad, Josh, and I play the dreidel game. We sit in a circle on the floor. Everyone gets five pieces of Hanukkah gelt. Dad puts three pieces of gelt in a pile in the middle of the circle. Then we take turns spinning the dreidel. On my first turn, the dreidel lands on the Hebrew letter nun, so I get nothing. But on my next turn, the dreidel lands on the letter gimel. That means I take the whole pile! Soon I win the game.

The Dreidel Song

I have a lit-tle drei-del, I made it out of clay. And

when it's dry and rea-dy, Then drei-del I shall play.

1

I have a little dreidel,

I made it out of clay.

 And when it's dry and ready,

Then dreidel I shall play.

2

I'll take my little dreidel

And give it a good strong spin.

I hope it lands on gimel,

For then I'm sure to win.

3

If I spin hay, I take half,

But none if I spin nun.

I get the pot with gimel,

With shin I must pay one.

MAKING A DREIDEL

Ancient dreidels may have been made out of clay. But you can make a dreidel out of all sorts of materials. Here is an easy one to make.

MATERIALS: square piece of cardboard (about 4" x 4"), pencil, marker, ruler

1. Use the ruler to draw lines from corner to corner on the piece of cardboard, dividing the cardboard into four triangles.

2. In each triangle, write one of the Hebrew letters.

נ   ג   ה   שׁ

nun   gimel   hay   shin

3. Poke a small hole in the center of the cardboard. Then push the pencil partway through the middle of the cardboard, letting it stick out about one inch. Spin the dreidel on the pencil point.

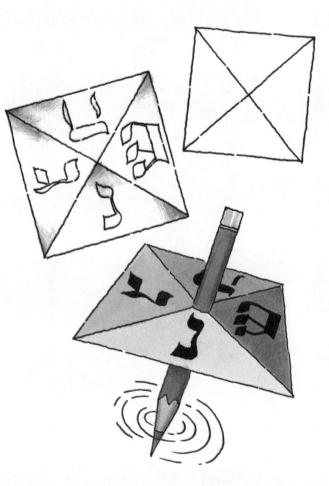

PLAYING THE DREIDEL GAME

A dreidel is a four-sided top. Each side has a Hebrew letter—nun, gimel, hay, or shin—on it. The letters stand for *Nes Gadol Hayah Sham*, which means "A Great Miracle Happened There." The letters also stand for the Yiddish words that explain how to play the game.

1. Give each player five chips, using gelt, pennies, or peanuts. Put several chips in a pile in the middle.

2. Take turns spinning the dreidel.

3. The letter that faces up when the dreidel stops tells the player what to do:
   נ Nun—*nisht* ("nothing"): **Take nothing.**
   ג Gimel—*gantz* ("everything"): **Take everything.**
   ה Hay—*halb* ("half"): **Take half.**
   ש Shin—*shtel* ("put in"): **Put one into the pile.**

4. If the pile is empty, or has only one chip, each player puts in one chip before the next spin.

5. Play until one player wins everything and the other players have nothing.

The Sixth Night

Tonight is the sixth night of Hanukkah. Grandma Sarah and Grandpa Lou come over with their arms full of presents. First we light the candles on the menorah. Then we open the presents! I get a soccer ball and a bead-making kit. Josh gets a basketball and a building toy. We surprise Grandma and Grandpa when they see that we have presents for them, too.

They love the picture frames we made!

MAKING A STAR-OF-DAVID PICTURE FRAME

MATERIALS: 6 popsicle sticks, glue, blue paint, paintbrush, glitter, a small photo of yourself, scissors, tape, yarn

1. Glue three sticks to form a triangle. Make a second triangle with the other three sticks. Then glue the triangles together to form a Star of David.

2. Mix a little glue into the paint and paint the frame blue. Before the paint dries, sprinkle glitter on the frame.

3. Cut the photo so that it fits inside the center of the star. Tape the photo to the back of the frame.

4. Loop a piece of yarn through the top of the frame and tie a knot at the top so that the picture can be hung.

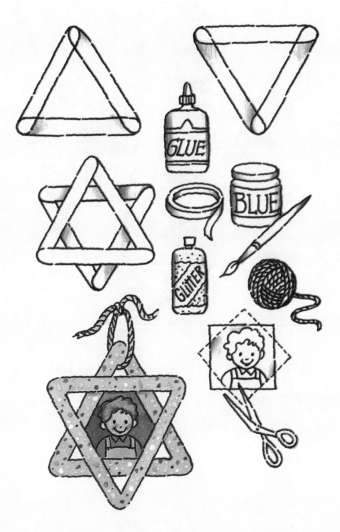

The Seventh Night

Tonight is the seventh night of Hanukkah. When we light the candles this time, we're a little sad. Hanukkah is almost over! Josh and I put on a play for Mom and Dad about the Maccabees. I make my costume and help Josh make his. He is Judah the Maccabee, and I am one of his soldiers.

MAKING A MACCABEE SHIELD

MATERIALS: piece of cardboard (about 11" x 11"), scissors, aluminum foil, tape, blue construction paper, glue, strip of cardboard (about 1 1/2" x 6")

1. Cut a large circle out of the cardboard square. You can use a dinner plate to trace the outline of a circle.

2. Cover the circle with aluminum foil. Fold the edges over to the back of the cardboard and tape down the foil.

3. Cut six strips of blue construction paper, about 1"x 9". Use the strips to form two triangles, making a Star of David. Glue them onto the front of the shield.

4. To form the handle, bend the 6" strip of cardboard up in the middle. Tape the ends to the back of the shield.

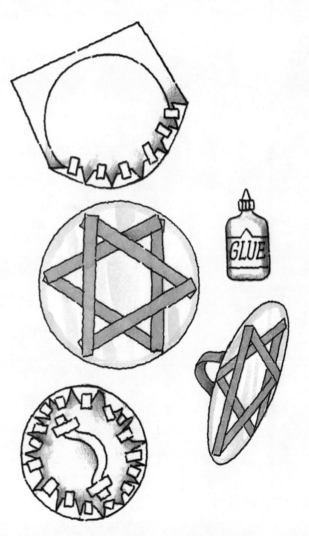

The Maccabee Song

The Eighth Night

Tonight is the last night of Hanukkah. We're having company again, and Josh and I are busy making cards for everyone. My favorite one is in the shape of a dreidel.

After our friends and relatives arrive, we light the candles. We exchange cards and presents. Soon Hanukkah is over. I miss it already. I can't wait until Hanukkah comes again next year!

MAKING HANUKKAH CARDS

MATERIALS: construction paper, scissors, markers, crayons, glue, glitter, assorted materials such as yarn, pipe cleaners, colored tissue paper, and craft gems

1. Cut out a piece of construction paper twice the size you want your card to be. Then fold the construction paper in half. If you want, cut the card in the shape of a dreidel, Star of David, or candle, using the patterns shown here.

2. Use markers, crayons, glitter, yarn, pipe cleaners, and any other materials you wish to decorate the front of your card. Then decorate the inside of the card and write a message.

HANUKKAH CONCENTRATION

Play this matching game with your friends and family during your Hanukkah celebration. Cut out the cards. Mix them up and place them face down in rows. Take turns flipping over two cards to find a match. You have a match when a "numeral" card equals the number of lit candles on a "menorah" card. If you have a match, you keep the two cards. If you don't have a match, turn the cards over again and let the next player take a turn.

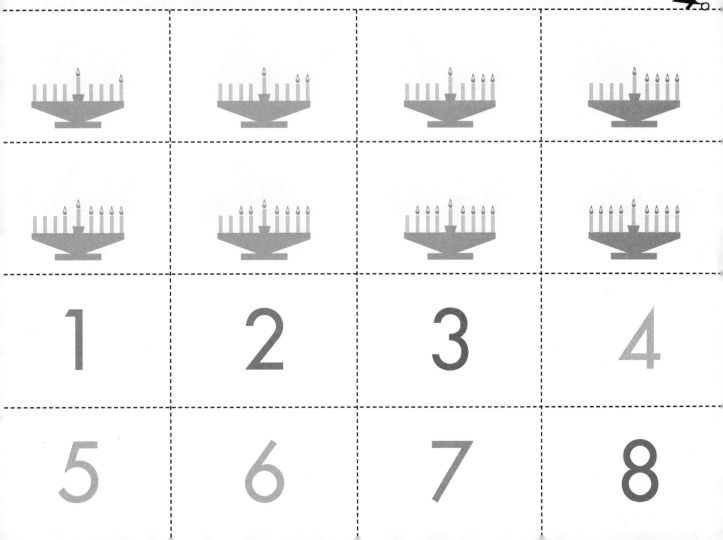